ETUDE ON "10,000 REASONS" ("BLESS THE LORD")

Music by Jonas Myrin and Matt Redman
Arranged by TIMOTHY SHAW

© Copyright 2011 Shout! Music Publishing (APRA) (admin. in the US and Canada by CapitolCMGPublishing) / Thankyou Music (PRS) (admin. worldwide by CapitolCMGPublishing excluding Europe which is admin. by Integritymusic.com) / Worshiptogether.com Songs (ASCAP) / Sixsteps Music (ASCAP) (admin. by CapitolCMGPublishing). All rights reserved. Used by permission.

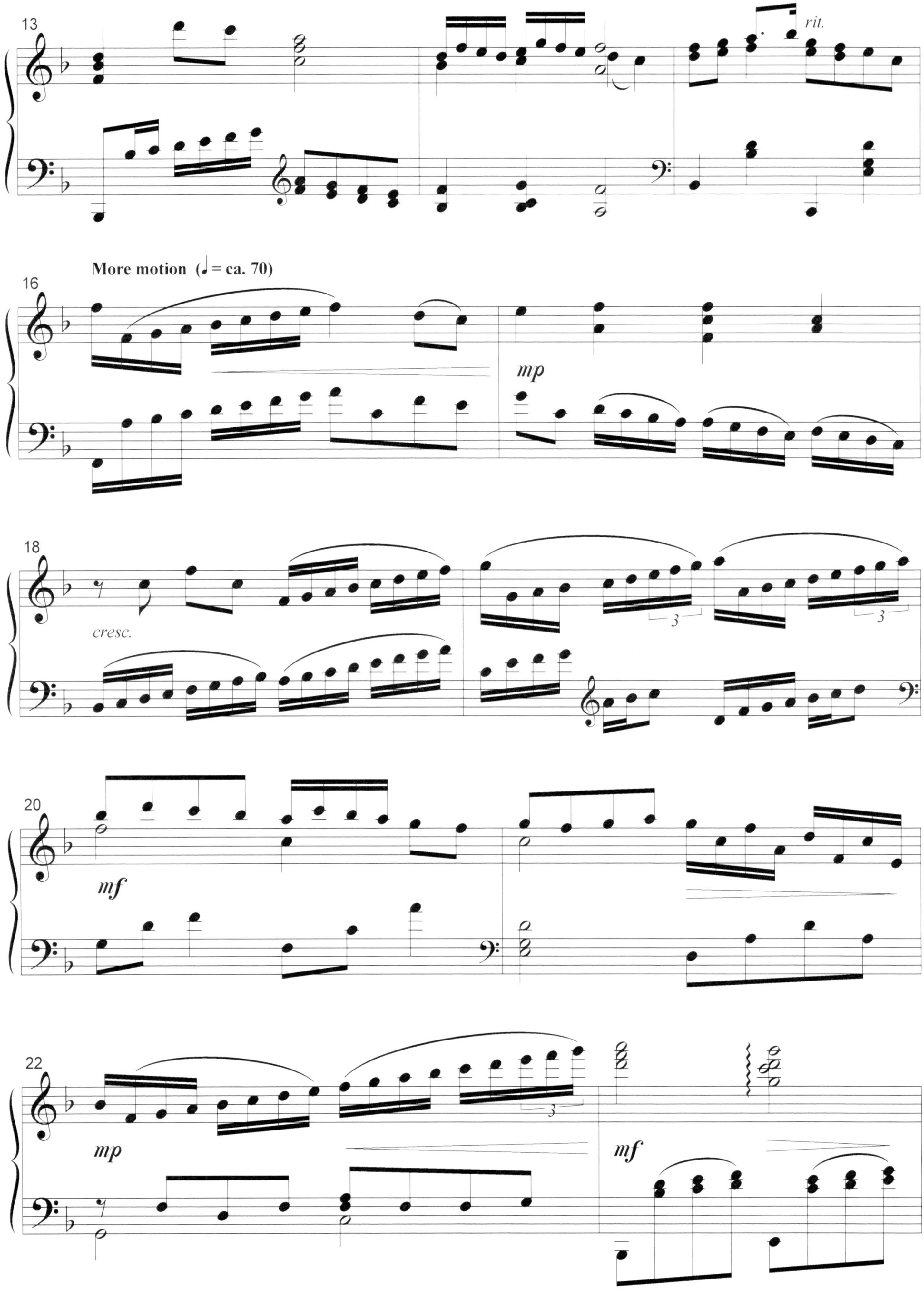
13
rit.
More motion (♩ = ca. 70)
16
mp
18
cresc.
3
3
20
mf
22
mp
3
mf

24
rit.
Tempo I
mp
mp
27
30
rit.
33
More motion (♩ = ca. 70)
mf
36
espressivo
dim.
mp

39
rit.
42
a tempo
p
mf
44
f
mf
8vb
46
rall.
(8vb)
p legato
49

52
55
mp
cresc.
Tempo I
58
rit.
f
60
62
8vb

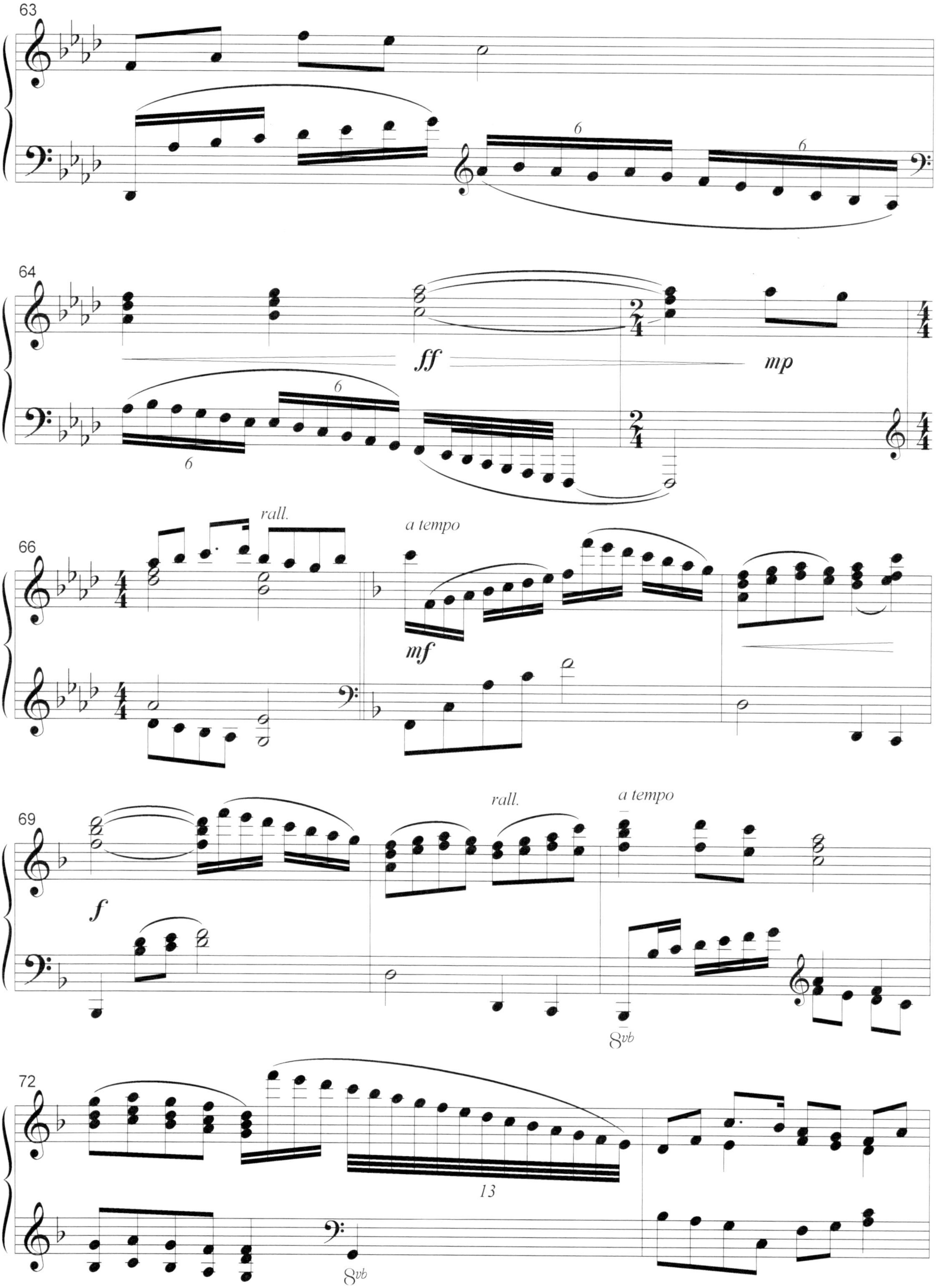
63
6
6
64
ff
mp
6
66
rall.
a tempo
mf
69
f
rall.
a tempo
8vb
72
13
8vb

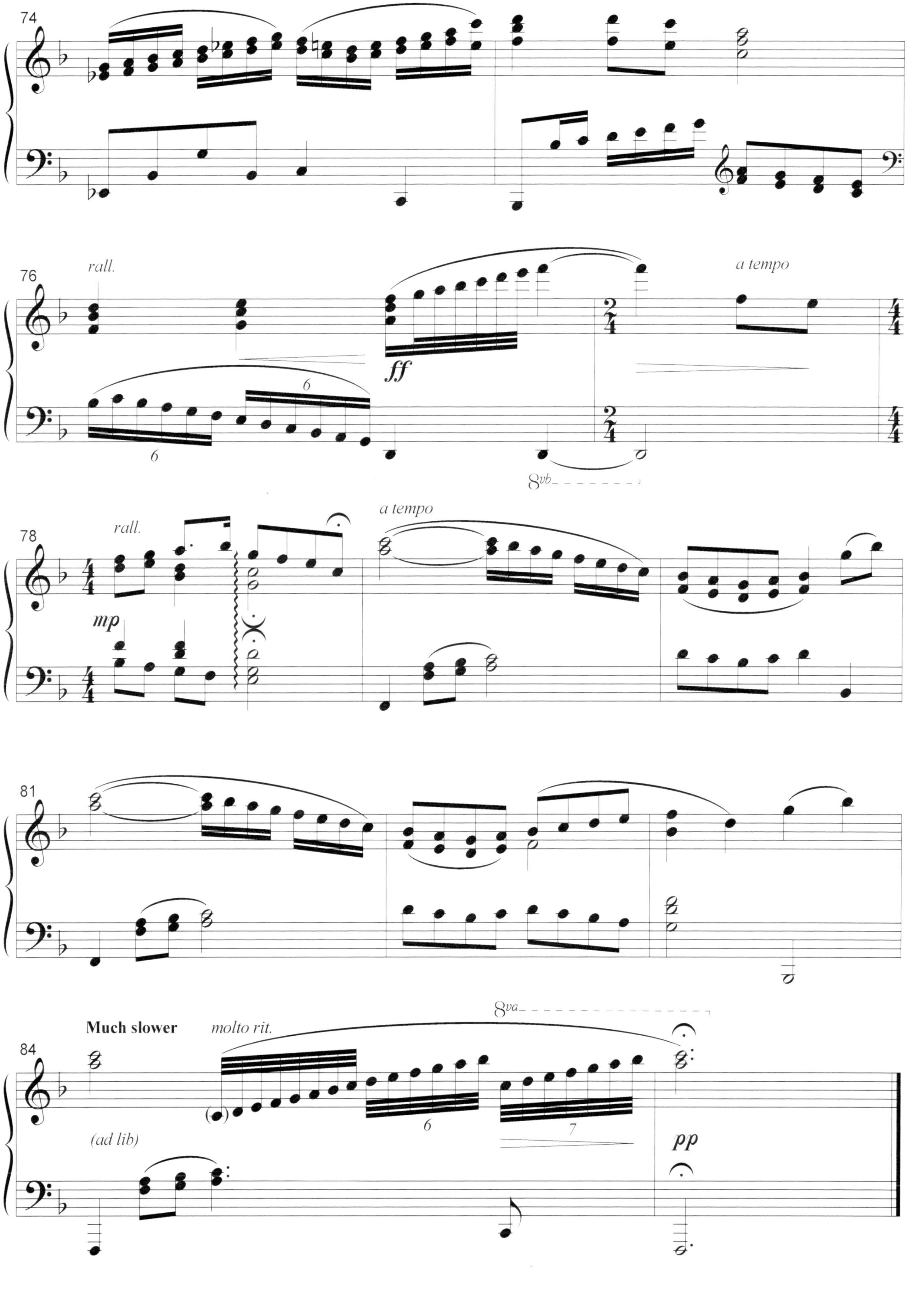
74
76
rall.
6
6
ff
a tempo
8vb
78
rall.
mp
a tempo
81
84
Much slower
molto rit.
8va
(ad lib)
6
7
pp